FIFTY-FIVE PIECES OF GOLD

MOVIES / TV BROADWAY

FOLK / SOUL

POP / ROCK

AS LONG AS HE NEEDS ME

Words and Music by
LIONEL BART

BLESS THE BEASTS AND CHILDREN

Words and Music by
BARRY DE VORZON and PERRY BOTKIN, JR.

BRIAN'S SONG

Piano Solo

Arranged by SID ENGEL

Music by
MICHEL LEGRAND

CONSIDER YOURSELF

Words and Music by
LIONEL BART

Moderate march tempo

FLY ME TO THE MOON
(IN OTHER WORDS)

Words and Music by
BART HOWARD

FOR ALL WE KNOW

Music by
FRED KARLIN

Lyrics by
ROBB WILSON and ARTHUR JAMES

ONE TIN SOLDIER

Words and Music by
DENNIS LAMBERT and BRIAN POTTER

Moderately Slow Rock Tempo

Verse

1. Lis - ten child - ren to a sto - ry that was writ - ten long a - go
2. So the peo - ple of the val - ley sent a mes - sage up the hill
3. Now the val - ley cried with an - ger mount your hors - es, draw your sword

'bout a king - dom on a moun - tain and the val - ley folk be - low.
ask - ing for the bur - ied trea - sure tons of gold for which they'd kill.
and they killed the moun - tain peo - ple so they won their just re - ward.

22

GONNA BUILD A MOUNTAIN

Music and Lyrics by
LESLIE BRICUSSE and ANTHONY NEWLEY

Grandioso

EXTRA VERSES

5.

Gonna build a heaven from a little hell
Gonna build a heaven and I know well
With a fine young son who will take my place
There'll be a sun in my heaven on earth
With the good Lord's grace.

6.

Gonna build a mountain from a little hill.
Gonna build a mountain — least I hope I will.
Gonna build a mountain — gonna build it high.
I don't know how I'm gonna do it
I only know I'm gonna try.

HAWAII FIVE-O

Words and Music
By MORT STEVENS

THE LOOK OF LOVE

Lyrics by
HAL DAVID
Music by
BURT BACHARACH

MRS. ROBINSON

Words and Music by
PAUL SIMON

SCARBOROUGH FAIR/CANTICLE

Arrangement and Original
Counter melody by
PAUL SIMON and ARTHUR GARFUNKEL

SING

Words and Music by
JOE RAPOSO

44

THE SOUND OF SILENCE

Words and Music by
PAUL SIMON

WHAT KIND OF FOOL AM I?

Words and Music by
LESLIE BRICUSSE and ANTHONY NEWLEY

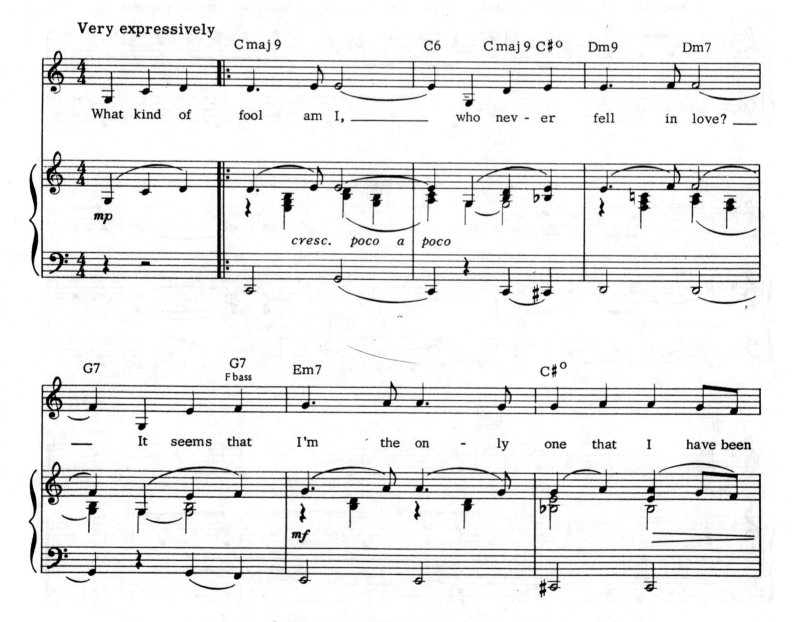

What kind of fool am I, _____ who nev-er fell in love? ___

It seems that I'm the on-ly one that I have been

PAUL SIMON BOOKS

THE SONGS OF PAUL SIMON

Includes all the songs made famous by Simon and Garfunkel and Paul Simon alone —
59 songs in all — has already sold over 200,000 -- point-of-purchase counter displays still available.

SOFT BOUND $6.95   HARD BOUND $12.95

PAUL SIMON

Includes the hits MOTHER AND CHILD REUNION, ME AND JULIO DOWN BY THE
SCHOOLYARD, and DUNCAN.

$3.95

PAUL SIMON — THERE GOES RHYMIN' SIMON

Matches the gold album — contains KODACHROME, AMERICAN TUNE,
LOVES ME LIKE A ROCK, a total of 10 songs, 80 pages. An obvious winner.

$4.50

THE SIMON AND GARFUNKEL GREATEST HITS SERIES

These books match the million plus selling album. Contents include: BRIDGE OVER
TROUBLED WATER, THE SOUND OF SILENCE, EL CONDOR PASA, SCARBOROUGH
FAIR/CANTICLE, MRS. ROBINSON, CECILIA, THE BOXER, plus seven more.

ARRANGED FOR
SIMON AND GARFUNKEL'S GREATEST HITS   piano/vocal/guitar $3.95

AIN'T NO SUNSHINE

Words and Music by
BILL WITHERS

Copyright © 1971 by INTERIOR MUSIC
Made in U.S.A.

EL CONDOR PASA (IF I COULD)

Musical Arrangement by
JORGE MILCHBERG and DANIEL ROBLES
English Lyric by
PAUL SIMON

sound,   its sad-dest sound.__

I'd rath-er be a for-est than a

street.   Yes I would.   If I could,__ I sure-ly would.__

I'd rath-er feel the earth be-neath my

feet.   Yes I would.   If I on-ly could,__ I sure-ly would.__

COUNTRY ROAD

Words and Music by
JAMES TAYLOR

feel it

on a coun-try road.

I guess my feet ____ know where they want me to go ____

walk-ing on a coun-try road. ___

D.S. %

Coda

Walk on down,_ walk on _ down, walk on down,_ walk on _ down, walk-ing on a coun-try road.

La la la la_ la la la la la la_ la la_

la la la la la la la la la_ la la la la_ Coun-try road_

Walk-ing on a coun-try road.

Repeat and fade

Coun-try road_

GHETTO CHILD

Words and Music by
THOM BELL and LINDA CREED

IF I HAD A HAMMER
(THE HAMMER SONG)

Words and Music by
LEE HAYS and PETE SEEGER

Moderately

1. If I Had A Ham-mer,—   I'd ham-mer in the morn - ing,—
2. (If I had a) bell,   I'd ring it in the morn - ing,—
3. (If I had a) song,   I'd sing it in the .morn - ing,—
4. Well, I got a) ham-mer,—   And I've got a bell, _____

I'd ham-mer in the eve - ning__   all o - ver this
I'd ring it in the eve - ning__   all o - ver this
I'd sing it in the eve - ning__   all o - ver this
And I've_ got a song   all o - ver this

LEAN ON ME

Words and Music by
BILL WITHERS

Moderately slow

72

MORNING HAS BROKEN

Words by
ELEANOR FARJEON
Musical Arrangement by
CAT STEVENS

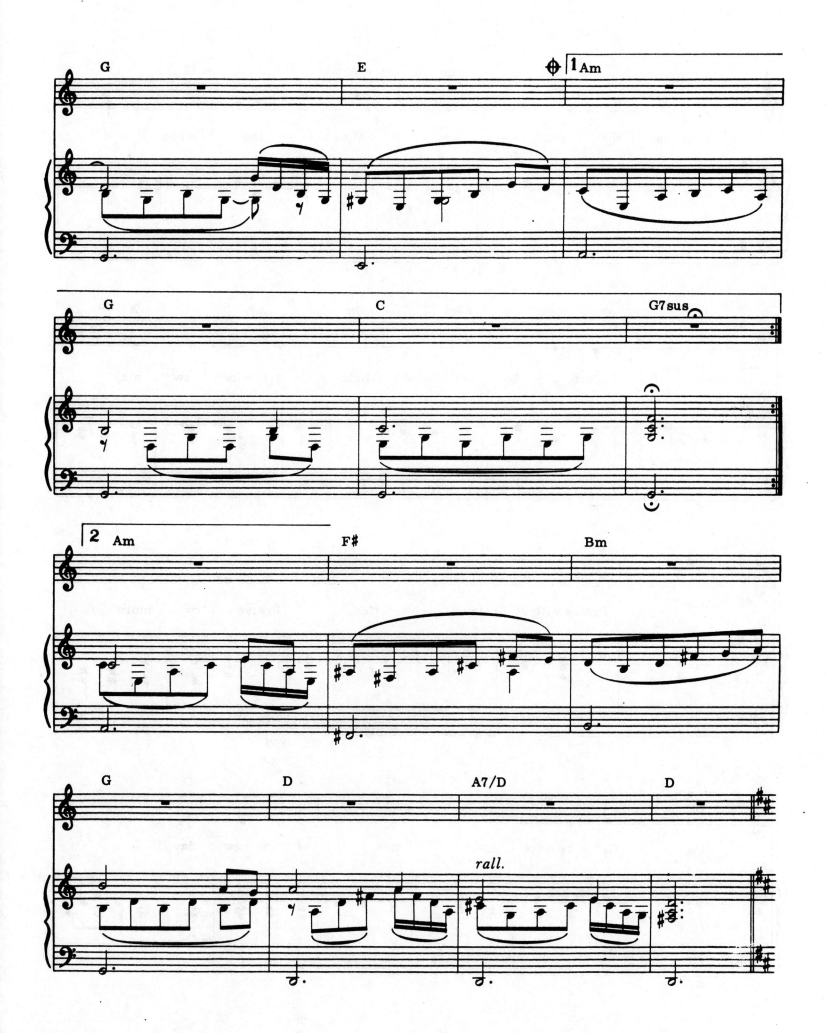

76

MR. BOJANGLES

Words and Music by
JERRY JEFF WALKER

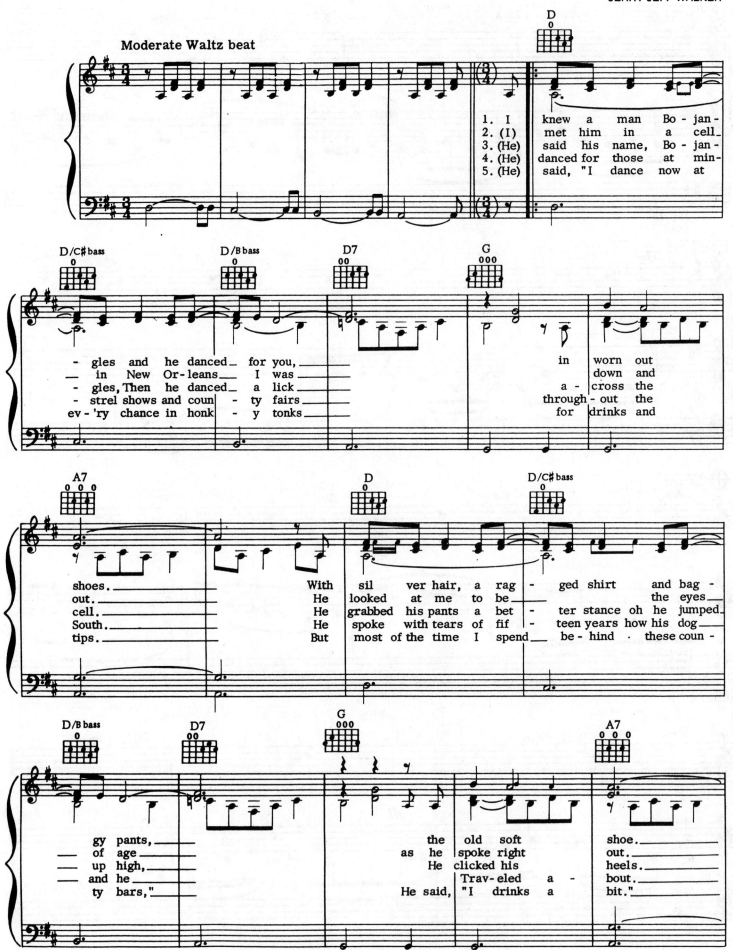

THIS LAND IS YOUR LAND

Words and Music by WOODY GUTHRIE
Additional Lyrics as sung by
PETE SEEGER

1. as i was walk - ing ——— that rib - bon of high - way ———
2. i've roamed and ram - bled ——— and i fol - lowed my foot - steps ———
3. when the sun comes shin - ing ——— and i was stroll - ing ———

— i saw a - bove me ——— that end - less sky - way ———
— to the spark - ling sands of ——— her dia - mond des - erts ———
— and the wheat - fields wav - ing ——— and the dust clouds roll - ing ———

— i saw be - low me ——— that gold - en val - ley ———
— and all a - round me ——— a voice was sound - ing ———
— as the fog was lift - ing ——— a voice was chant - ing ———

this land was made for you and me. ——— this land is

additional lyrics

was a big high wall there that tried to stop me;
a big sign painted said, "private property."
but on the back side it didn't say nothing except:
this land is made for you and me!

one bright sunday morning in the shadows of the steeple
by the relief office i seen my people;
as they stood there hungry, i stood there whistling:
this land is made for you and me.

ME AND MRS. JONES

Words and Music by
KENNY GAMBLE, LEON HUFF, and CARY GILBERT

TURN! TURN! TURN!
(TO EVERYTHING THERE IS A SEASON)

Words: Book Of Ecclesiastes
Adaptation and Music by
PETE SEEGER

AMERICAN TUNE

Words and Music by
PAUL SIMON

CALIFORNIA DREAMIN'

Words and Music by
JOHN PHILLIPS and MICHELLE PHILLIPS

94

AUBREY

Words and Music by
DAVID GATES

Cmaj7
G
(D Bass)
Gmaj7
Am7
G
(B Bass)
For the hearts_ that nev - er played in tune, like a love - ly mel - o - dy_ that ev -
If it did,_ it nev - er made a sound. May - be I_ was ab - sent or_ was lis -
C
G
(B Bass) c
Am7
G
(B Bass)
'ry - one can sing. Take a - way_ the words_ that rhyme,_ it
ten - ing too fast, Catch - ing all_ the words_ but then_ the
C
C#m7-5
Am
(D Bass)
D7sus
D7
C
C#m7-5
1.
2.
does - n't mean_ a thing.
mean - ing go - ing past.
G
(D Bass)
B7
(D# Bass)
Em
And God,_ I miss_ the girl_ And I'd go_
Oh, how_ I miss_ the girl_ And I'd go_

BRIDGE OVER TROUBLED WATER

Words and Music by
PAUL SIMON

Moderato, not too fast, like a spiritual

Rubato

When you're wea - ry, ___ feel - in' _____ small,
down and out, ___ When you're on the street,

When tears are in your eyes, ___ I'll dry .them_ all;
When eve - ning falls so hard ___ I will com - fort_ you. _____

DANIEL

Words and Music by
ELTON JOHN and BERNIE TAUPIN

1.4. Dan-iel is trav-'ling to-night__ on a 'plane__
2. They say Spain is pret - ty 'though I've nev-er been__
3. Instrumental ad lib. at 1st. D.S. (small notes)

I can see   the   red__ tail - lights__
Well Dan-iel   says__ it's the best__ place   he's

107

DON'T LET ME
BE LONELY TONIGHT

Words and Music by
JAMES TAYLOR

FIRE AND RAIN

Words and Music by
JAMES TAYLOR

IF

Words and Music by
DAVID GATES

GOODBYE TO LOVE

Lyrics by
JOHN BETTIS

Music by
RICHARD CARPENTER

I'M COMING HOME

Words and Music by
THOM BELL and LINDA CREED

*Guitarists: Tune 6th string to D

IT NEVER RAINS
IN SOUTHERN CALIFORNIA

Words and Music by
ALBERT HAMMOND and MIKE HAZELWOOD

JOY TO THE WORLD

Words and Music by
HOYT AXTON

Moderate Gospel Rock

1. Je-re-mi-ah was a bull-
(2.) If I were the
(3.) know I love the la-

-frog, Was a good friend of mine.
king of the world. Tell you what I'd do.
-dies, Love to have my fun. I'm a

Nev-er un-der-stood a sin-gle word he said,___ But I helped him a-drink-in' his wine.
Throw a-way the cars and the bars and the wars, And make sweet love to you.___
high night fly-er and a rain-bow ri-der, A straight shoot-in' son-of-a-gun.

Yes he al-ways had some might-y fine wine.
Yes I'd make sweet love to you.___
Yes a straight shoot-in' son-of-a-gun.___ Sing-ing

© Copyright 1970 by LADY JANE MUSIC, c/o MITCHELL, SILBERBERG & KNUPP, 1800 Century Park East, Los Angeles, California 90067
This arrangement © Copyright 1971 by LADY JANE MUSIC
International Copyright Secured   Made In U.S.A.   All Rights Reserved

128

LIGHT MY FIRE

Words and Music by
THE DOORS

With a beat

THE LION SLEEPS TONIGHT
(WIMOWEH) (MBUBE)

New Lyrics and Revised Music by
HUGO PERETTI, LUIGI CREATORE
GEORGE WEISS, and ALBERT STANTON
Based on a Song by
SOLOMON LINDA and PAUL CAMPBELL

NEVER BEEN TO SPAIN

Words and Music by
HOYT AXTON

Rock Blues Feel

1. Well I Nev - er Been To Spain___ but I kind - a like the

4. *(instrumental ad lib)* ___

mu - sic. I hear the la - dies are in - sane there and they sure know how to

use it. They don't a - buse it. They'll nev - er

lose it. I can't re - fuse it. 2. Well, I Nev - er Been To
___ *(fade out)* ___

135

PAPER ROSES

Lyrics by JANICE TORRE
Music by FRED SPIELMAN

RAINY DAYS AND MONDAYS

Music by
ROGER NICHOLS

Lyrics by
PAUL WILLIAMS

Moderately Slow

1. Talk-in' to my-self and feel-in' old,
2. What I've got they used to call the blues,
3. What I feel has come and gone be - fore,

some-times I'd like to quit, no - thing ev - er seems to fit. Hang- in' a-round,
noth-in' is real-ly wrong, feel-in' like I don't be-long. Walk-in' a-round,
no need to talk it out, we know what it's all a- bout. Hang- in' a-round,

SHAMBALA

Words and Music by
DANIEL MOORE

143

144

SO FAR AWAY

Words and Music by
CAROLE KING

SLIGHTLY OUT OF TUNE
(DESAFINADO)

English Lyrics by
JON HENDRICKS and JESSIE CAVANAUGH

Music by
ANTONIO CARLOS JOBIM

Original Text by
NEWTON MENDOÇA

SPINNING WHEEL

Words and Music by
DAVID C. THOMAS

SWEET BABY JAMES

Words and Music by
JAMES TAYLOR

YOU'VE GOT A FRIEND

Words and Music by
CAROLE KING

THOSE WERE THE DAYS

Words and Music by
GENE RASKIN

TIE A YELLOW RIBBON
ROUND THE OLE OAK TREE

Words and Music by
IRWIN LEVINE and L. RUSSELL BROWN

1. I'm com - in' home,___ I've done my time,___ now I've
2. Bus driv - er please___ look for me,___ 'cause I

got to know___ what is___ and is - n't mine.___ If
could - n't bear___ to see___ what I might see.___ I'm

WAS A SUNNY DAY

Words and Music by
PAUL SIMON

A WHITER SHADE OF PALE

Words and Music by
KEITH REID and GARY BROOKER

I was feel-ing kind of sea - sick
So I took her by the look-ing glass
But I wan-dered through my play-ing cards

The crowd called out
And forced her to
And would not let

— for more
— a - gree
— her be

The room was hum - ming hard -
Say - ing, "You must be the mer -
One of six - teen ves - tal vir -

— er
— maid
— gins

As the ceil - ing flew a - way,
Who took Nep-tune for a ride,"
Who were leav-ing for the coast,

When we called out for an - oth - er drink
But she smiled at me so sad - ly
And al- though my eyes were o - pen

WE'VE ONLY JUST BEGUN

Music by
ROGER NICHOLS

Lyrics by
PAUL WILLIAMS

1. We've On-ly Just Be-gun to live, White lace and
2. Be-fore the ris-ing sun we fly, So man-y
3. And when the eve-ning comes we smile, So much of

prom-i-ses A kiss for luck and we're on our way.
roads to choose We start out walk-ing and learn to run.
life a-head We'll find a place where there's room to grow,

And yes, We've Just Be-gun.

Shar-ing hor-i-zons that are

YESTERDAY WHEN I WAS YOUNG
(HIER ENCORE)

Original French Text and Music by CHARLES AZNAVOUR
English Lyrics by HERBERT KRETZMER

180